SEW HILARIOUS

MARY A. ROEHR

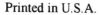

W9-BVN-452

DEDICATED TO THE SEWERS OF THE WORLD:

THE ONLY PEOPLE WHO CAN DO SOMETHING

INSIDE OUT, UPSIDE DOWN, AND BACKWARDS,

AND HAVE IT TURN OUT RIGHT!

TABLE OF CONTENTS

CHAPTER 1

LEARNING TO SEW

SEWING TEACHERS OF THE PAST

"I DIDN'T KNOW YOU HAD TO PRESHRINK THE FABRIC *BEFORE* YOU SEW IT!"

ALWAYS STRAIGHTEN THE GRAIN!

"I WONDERED WHY THE NOTCHES DIDN'T MATCH!"

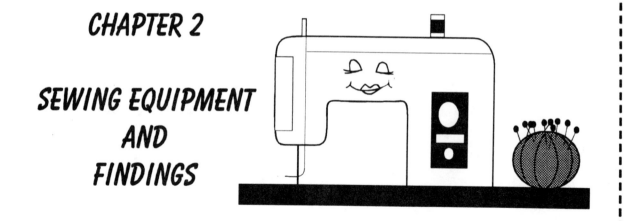

CHAPTER 2

SEWING EQUIPMENT
AND
FINDINGS

SEWING MACHINES OF THE FUTURE

THE ULTIMATE MONOGRAMMING MACHINE

14

KEEPING UP WITH THE JONESES IN THE SERGER NEIGHBORHOOD

SEWING MACHINE SOAP OPERAS

"I THOUGHT THE **IRON AGE** WAS OVER!"

AUTOMATIC TAPE MEASURE

18

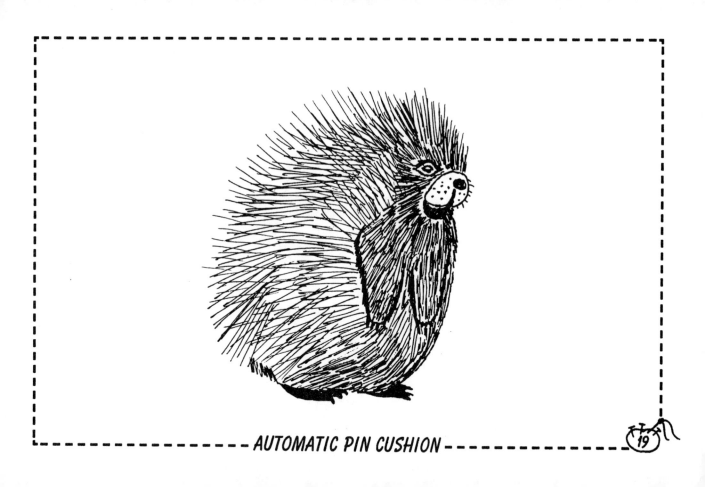

AUTOMATIC PIN CUSHION

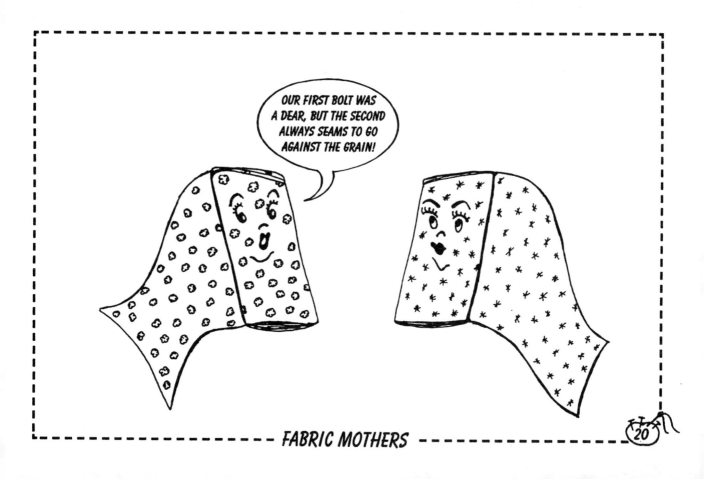

FABRIC MOTHERS

CHAPTER 3

GENERAL SEWING

SUPER SEWER

"I WISH YOU'D SHOW THIS MUCH ENTHUSIASM ON THE DANCE FLOOR!"

THE SEWING SECRETARY

"WHERE I COME FROM, PIECING MEANT EATING BETWEEN MEALS!"

THERE ONCE WAS A LADY FROM MAINE,

WHO LIKED TO SEW AND COMPLAIN.

SHE'D TAKE OUT HER THREAD,

PUT HER HANDS TO HER HEAD,

AND EXCLAIM, "OH, MY, WHAT A PAIN!"

27

"THE FIT OF THE BODICE IS IN DIRECT PROPORTION TO YOUR AGE:
FOR EVER 5 YEARS OVER 30, LOWER THE BUST DART 1 INCH!"

"I HAVE A FIGURE LIKE AN HOURGLASS-
TIME JUST STOPPED IN THE WRONG PLACES!"

30

MY WALKING FOOT IS ALWAYS BROKEN.

MY FEED DOGS ARE ALWAYS HUNGRY.

MY PRESSURE FOOT IS ALWAYS LOOSE.

MY THREAD TENSION IS ALWAYS HIGH.

MY NEEDLE THREADER IS ALWAYS LOOPED.

MY STITCH LENGTH IS NEVER REGULATED,
AND MY CONTROL PANEL IS OUT OF CONTROL.

NO WONDER I CAN NEVER GET ANYTHING DONE!

CHAPTER 4

SEWING AS THERAPY

"I'M REALLY WORRIED ABOUT SALLY, SHE TOLD ME JUST THE OTHER DAY THAT SHE DOESN'T HAVE A STASH ANYMORE!"

33

DR. BROWN

SEWER'S E.K.G.

35

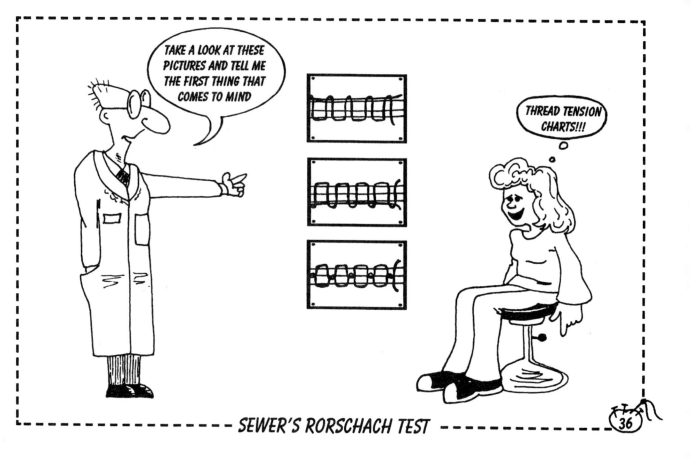

SEWER'S RORSCHACH TEST

LINDA FINDS HER PURPOSE

37

CHAPTER 5

SEWING GETAWAYS

It's Vacation Time!

ATTENTION

LIFEBOAT DRILL

— SEWER'S CRUISE —

39

SEWER'S BEACH VACATION

— SEWING SAFARI —

41

"I USED TO THINK GOING 6 BLOCKS
FOR A SPOOL OF THREAD WAS FAR!"

44

— THE GARMENT DISTRICT —

CHAPTER 6

SEWING FOR OTHERS

DRESSMAKER

47

"I JUST WANT A **SIMPLE** DRESS."

"I CAN'T WAIT MORE THAN 2 WEEKS OR
MY FOOD WILL RUN OUT."

50

"AT FIRST MY HUSBAND DIDN'T LIKE MY SEWING FOR OTHER PEOPLE, BUT I THINK HE'S ADJUSTED!"

"I THINK YOU FINALLY GOT A CUSTOMER!"

54

CHAPTER 7

THE LIFE OF A FABRIHOLIC

-FIRST YOU ONLY BUY FABRIC SOCIALLY...-

56

--- THEN YOU TRY TO GET OTHERS TO BUY FABRIC WITH YOU... - - - -

SOON YOU BECOME PREOCCUPIED WITH FABRIC...

58

YOU BECOME OUT OF CONTROL AND GO ON FABRIC BUYING BINGES...

YOU START HIDING FABRIC ALL OVER THE HOUSE...

FINALLY YOU GIVE UP EVERYTHING FOR YOUR FABRIC...

61